HAVE FAITH IN THE GOOD

BY

Herbert E. Thomas, M.D.

INTRODUCTION

By

Michael Hogan

"Have Faith In The Good," by Herbert E. Thomas, M.D. ISBN 978-1-60264-382-6. (Softcover) ISBN 978-1-60264-425-0 (Hardcover).

Library of Congress Control Number: 2011913431.

Published 2011 by Virtualbookworm.com Publishing Inc., P.O. Box 9949, College Station, TX 77842, US. ©2011, Herbert E. Thomas, M.D. All rights reserved. No part of this publication may be reproduced, stored in a retrieval system, or transmitted in any form or by any means, electronic, mechanical, recording or otherwise, without the prior written permission of Herbert E. Thomas, M.D.

Manufactured in the United States of America.

HAVE FAITH IN THE GOOD

By

Herbert E. Thomas, M.D.

To Barbara

INTRODUCTION

I first met Dr. Herbert Thomas 34 years ago when I was invited by John Paul Minarik to visit the Academy of Prison Arts Writers' Workshop at Western Penitentiary in Pittsburgh. The workshop, which was the first prisoner-organized program of its kind funded by the NEA, sought to bring experienced writers into the penal institution to work with prisoners. After the workshop was over, Dr. Thomas, who was the resident psychiatrist, arranged for me to also meet a prisoner who could not attend the workshop because of illness and was being held in a segregation cell. I was impressed by the doctor's compassion (rare enough in such settings) and his commitment to see that each inmate had a chance to participate in what few opportunities were available for rehabilitation. Dr. Thomas has since gone on to become a noted psychiatrist in private practice in New York as well as an author. His book "The Shame Response To Rejection" is used by

1

psychiatrists, clinical psychologists, educators and social workers. Yet, I remember him simply as a kind and compassionate man making a small gesture in a large and cold institution where such gestures were rare.

So, when I was sent a copy of the minimalist work on spirituality and asked by my old friend and fellow poet to write an introduction, I was excited but also a bit puzzled. Spirituality is not usually the province of modern psychology, although it should have a closer relationship as William James reminded us so brilliantly in his "Varieties of Religious Experience." Like James, Dr. Thomas's account is anecdotal. He relates experiences of what T. S. Eliot called "the intersection of the timeless with time."

Paul Éluard once wrote, "There is another world and it's in this one." That is the thesis to which Dr. Thomas subscribes, and his experiences assure him that it is not only true, but it is a sign that the other world is constantly interpenetrating this one and sending messages, chief of which is that we must have faith in the good, that the world is full of blessings. One delightful anecdote that Dr. Thomas relates has to do with the removal of a beautiful tree in a forest in Canada when he was a young man working on a surveying crew because the tree interfered with the line of sight necessary for measurement. He felt a deep sense of loss when he chopped down the tree and later a sense of shame as well that he had destroyed a thing more valuable than what he had put in its place: a survey marker for a mining company. Fifty years later, alone in the woods, the tree's spirit made itself known to him in a way that was unforgettable.

While this occurrence seems more in the vein of sentient Loren Eiseley than that of an acknowledged Christian, there are Christian precedents for this as well. "Brother Moon, Sister Sun" the famous poem by Francis of Assisi with its lively pantheistic lines was written by a Christian saint. Teresa of Avila also experienced many spiritual revelations through nature as did William Wordsworth who assured us that in nature there is a "Presence," which ensures that all "the dreary intercourse of daily life shall not prevail against us" and reminds us "all which we behold is full of blessings."

Later in this short work the good doctor travels to Jerusalem where he encounters human "messengers" who make him aware of this "incarnation" or the merging of the spirit world with the material one. These instances of transcendence are gifts of vision. They are flashes of illumination to which the sense of self, the ego, is suddenly held in abeyance and Dr. Thomas (and we the readers) feel that we are a part of something much larger.

Which brings me to the importance of this little book and why John Paul Minarik sought out a fellow poet to write the introduction to it. The anecdotes related here have the power, if we let them, to produce a corresponding illumination in the reader, an illumination in which the ordinary suddenly manifests itself as extraordinary, and everything is connected. It was John's hope that these moments related by Dr. Thomas might illuminate your life as they have ours, allowing you to experience these "moments in and out of time," which can release us – if we let them – from the tedious bondage of self.

–*Michael Hogan*
Guadalajara, Jalisco, Mexico
December 2010

Scots have told us that on the isle of Iona, the Holy Isle, off the west coast of Scotland, there is only a thin sheet that separates Heaven and Earth.

In Jerusalem nothing separates Heaven and Earth. Certain individuals traditionally known as angels and messengers pass back and forth between the two realities seemingly without hindrance.

PREFACE

H erbert E. Thomas, M.D. is a modern-day mystic who walks the spiritual journey together with all those who have gone before him down through the ages of time.

I first began to realize this truth as "Doc Thomas" became my mentor in prison ministry during the 1970-80's in Pittsburgh, Pennsylvania. Every week as we visited the men in the maximum security prison called Western Penitentiary, I always sensed there was "another presence" with us, and it was Doc Thomas who helped identify that spiritual mystery for all of us. Jesus said "Where two or three are gathered together in my name, I will be there in the midst of them" (Matthew 18:20). And it was His presence that we sensed and felt every time we entered into the prison.

I also experienced that presence in a very personal way when, after two spinal surgeries, Doc Thomas came to visit with me every week as I recovered. The gifts of his special friendship and abiding faith helped me get through "the dark night of the soul," and I will be forever thankful to him for the lessons he has taught me about life and learning to love one another as sisters and brothers in the human family.

Herb Thomas's new book "Have Faith in the Good" takes us on a profound journey from his birthplace in Canada, to his many years as a psychiatrist in prisons in Michigan and Pennsylvania, his remarkable work as a Park Avenue therapist in New York City, his travels to Tuscany, Jerusalem and other parts of Israel. The "spiritual companions" that he has met along the way and describes in the book help to reveal what the ancient Celtic people described as the "thin places" – otherworldly experiences where "close encounters of the spiritual kind" happen. Believing that all of us have been touched by similar "encounters," Doc Thomas helps us get in touch with those nearer to The Holy Presence.

This book is beautifully written from the heart and soul of a mentor and friend who has influenced more lives than could be possibly counted, and I hope that you will enjoy reading every chapter of this remarkable and inspiring journey.

–Dr. George B. Wirth
Senior Pastor
First Presbyterian Church
Atlanta, Georgia

AUTHOR'S PREFACE

T his is the story of one person's attempt to understand and to relate to another reality which surrounds each of us. The teaching of the three monotheistic religions are central to the understanding of this story, particularly Christianity and Judaism.

I believe that my work as a psychiatrist in caring for countless men in maximum security prisons, first in Michigan and then in Pennsylvania, has been the most important fact of my life. Many of them I still remember, and many events that occurred in those years are still very clear in my mind. Training in psychoanalysis helped me to better understand them and how we related to one another as significant others.

To say that my work was the most important fact of my life may come as a surprise to my family as I have been blessed with the most accepting and loving of wives. Our family consists of four children, their spouses and fifteen grandchildren all of whom we admire and love deeply. Both of us follow the progress of each of them with great attention and much cheering.

However, it was in prison work that I began to sense that there is another reality besides the one we experience. What follows is but one example of why I say this.

In the State Correctional Institution of Pittsburgh, previously called Western Penitentiary, there are two large rectangular cellblocks. Each has five tiers of cells placed back to back along the middle of the block. About thirty feet separate the catwalks, that front each tier, from the outside walls. The bottom tier of cells is at the level of the floor of the building, so it has no catwalk.

On one of my last days there, I was asked by the Superintendent to see an inmate in his cell. He was in the last cell on the top tier. After talking with him for a while, I retraced my steps along the catwalk which meant walking almost the full length of the block. As I did so flight after flight of noisy sparrows would swoop up beside me and then dive back down. This pattern was repeated five or six times as I walked along. As a parting salute, it was something I could never have imagined. This occurred in 1992.

My growing awareness of another reality is what I want to share with the reader.

The Celts thought of that reality as simply the otherworld which was as real to them as this one.

AN INTRODUCTION TO THE
OTHERWORLD OF THE CELTS

I begin by telling of an event that occurred in late July or early August of 1947 when I was eighteen years old. It was the summer following my graduation from the Royal Canadian Naval College at Royal Roads, British Columbia and beginning my sophomore year at McGill University in Montreal, Quebec.

A friend of my oldest sister, Alec Tate, owned an exploration company in northern Quebec and hired me as a surveyor's assistant for the summer. The base camp was on the eastern shore of Lake Albanel which is a good size lake. It is just east of a much larger one, Lake Mistassini, which is easily seen on a map east of James Bay. The Rupert River flows from Lake Mistassini into the southern-most corner of James Bay. At the time, I understood we were three hundred miles south of the Takwa mountains and the treeline.

We were located in a true wilderness. The nearest bush road was a hundred miles to the south of us which meant that access to the camp was by canoe or floatplane. No logging had ever occurred so that everywhere was virgin forest.

There were usually four members in our party when out in the woods. Jean de Sève was the surveyor and a Professor at the École Polytechnique in Montreal. There were two Cree Indians, the younger was René, and myself. Today the two native men would be called First Nation. They were from the Lake Saint John region.

René and I competed to see who could walk the fastest and carry the most, usually a little over a hundred pounds, using a tump line, when on long portages. As he usually won, it helped us become good friends. Before the summer was over, he asked if I would consider spending the coming winter with him hunting in the Takwa mountains.

Our work consisted of putting in claim lines to obtain the mineral rights to many square miles of forest. There was some evidence of hematite, an iron ore, in the area, but nothing was ever found worthy of being mined. A huge deposit was found east of us near the Labrador-Quebec border at about that time, so there was some interest in the mining community as to what we were doing.

When one puts in a claim line, to work the border of a claim, the surveyor first has to locate a permanent metal marker placed during a government survey. This is marked with the latitude and longitude and is very accurate. A point is then chosen in relation to it and this point marks the corner of the claim which has straight sides and must be staked out.

Initially a small straight tree is cut down, stripped of its branches and sharpened at both ends. It is then driven into the ground to mark the corner of the claim. A transit is then used to line up the next stake along the claim line, which is at least a hundred feet away, but this depends on the ups and downs of the forest floor. The next stake is lined up with the first two by looking back along the claim line, and so it continues until that line is completed.

Problems begin when one comes to swampy ground covered with brush or a particularly large tree. One day I was working alone and had put in quite a number of stakes, clearing out the brush between them. At one point looking back, I realized that my view was blocked by a tree that must have been three feet in diameter. At the time, I saw no other choice but to cut it down, which I did, even though it seemed terribly wasteful and left me very saddened. I went on with my work, but I never forgot the incident, and I feel sad to this day when I think about it.

Fifty years later, in the summer of 1997, I was confronted by what I will call the tree's spirit. It was asking why I had done such a terrible thing to it. Nothing could change what had happened, but it occurred to me I could offer to have it travel with me and that seemed to resolve our meeting. I did sense at several different times that it was accompanying me.

In February 2002, I flew Swiss Air to Tel Aviv by way of Zurich. The return took us over northern Quebec and as close to Lake Albanel as I was likely to get. During the night, as I was half dozing, I experienced what I can only describe as an excited rustling sound immediately behind me. It lasted for several moments, and then it was gone. I felt at peace and fell back to sleep.

There was one other experience with a tree that I can readily recall. I was driving from New York City to Pittsburgh on the Pennsylvania Turnpike and was west of the Carlisle Interchange. I stopped to take a break in a pull-off where there was a good-sized graveled area and a small wood. I was delighted to get out and get some air and bounded into the woods. In response to something I was saying aloud, I was cursed out: The words came to me from one of the trees! I was quite shocked, and it took a few minutes to get myself together.

I reviewed the situation and chose to look at the tree from different angles. From one angle I made out the figure of an old man. He reminded me strongly of Henri de Toulouse-Lautrec's man in the black suit in his poster of LaGoulue.

It is the presence of trees then that I associate with the otherworld of the Celts, but also birds.

EARLY YEARS

I was born in 1928 and was raised in the City of Quebec, the capitol of the Province of Quebec. Our family attended the Cathedral of the Holy Trinity, the church of the Anglican Bishop of Quebec. It has a long and interesting history as it was built sometime after the battle of the Plains of Abraham which was fought in September, 1759. Growing up, I came to idealize both General Montcalm and General Wolfe who had been commanders of the French and British troops.

There is a small park behind the Chateau Frontenac, a famous hotel close to the Cathedral, in which a monument to both Wolfe and Montcalm can be found. The name Wolfe and the name Montcalm are on opposite sides, and there are no other words. It has always symbolized for me my deeply felt admiration for both French and English Quebecers.

The Cathedral is interesting for many reasons. For one, it was designed to resemble the Church of St. Martin's in the Fields in

14

London, England. There is a stained glass window above the altar which shows the ascension of Jesus Christ in beautiful color. The red of His robe is brilliant. Also there is a special box in the north balcony for the use of the King and Queen when visiting Quebec. I recall them seated in the box when they visited in the spring of 1939 before the war broke out in September.

It was in the church that I had a visual hallucination. I was probably twelve or thirteen, and it happened on a Sunday morning when my mother and father were there. I do not believe any of my three sisters were present.

I saw two dark figures, both men. One was seated in a chair, and the other was standing behind him with his hand on the first man's shoulder. The scene lasted only a few seconds. I never mentioned this to anyone. I have never had a hallucination at any other time in my life.

Another event occurred about that same time which I well remember. I was delivering a letter to a Jewish family who lived a block away. It was Friday evening, so Shabbat had already begun. When I rang the doorbell, it was answered by one of the family whom I could see seated in a circle in the living room. One of them was reading to the others, and I was struck by the warmth of their being together. I was asked to come in, but I declined to do so.

I have many fond memories of childhood. Summers were spent at Lake Beauport about twelve miles north of Quebec in the Laurentian mountains. There were many hours spent swimming and playing with a brother and sister who lived nearby. However, the two events mentioned above seem to stand out in my memory.

I graduated from the Quebec High School in 1945 at age sixteen and went to the Royal Canadian Naval College located outside of Esquimalt, British Columbia. It was a two year college program leading to the rank of Midshipman. Graduation was in June, 1947, and I entered the Royal Canadian Navy (Reserve). From that time on I had two careers. One was in the reserve navy, and the other was attending pre-med and then medical school. The latter was at Queen's University in Kingston, Ontario.

As to Quebec, my father died in 1955 and my mother in 1972. The house was sold in 1972, and the one sister who had lived with her moved to Montreal, so there was little reason to visit the city other than to visit Mount Hermon Cemetery.

In 1949, I served as a Sub-Lieutenant in H.M.C.S. Beacon Hill, a frigate, where most of the officers had been in the war and had been in convoys in the North Atlantic. They were a great bunch and could not have been more supportive of a neophyte. I had spent the previous summer as a deckhand in the S.S. Imperial Winnipeg, an oil tanker, sailing to South America, so I had at least some sense of the enormous help the petty officers could be.

The 'Beacon Hill' was berthed at Esquimalt which is just outside of Victoria, British Columbia, so many of the officers came from the Prairie Provinces. Two of them, one a watch-keeping type, and the other, the supply officer, were devout Christians. The former made it clear he was born again whereas the latter was an Anglican priest who taught at the University of Toronto and was more conservative. Both men I found to be very genuine and more than willing to share their own views with me as to their Christian beliefs. Before the summer ended, I made a promise to follow Jesus Christ. I felt it was final and never thought of revoking my promise.

THE MYSTICAL WORLD

I choose to write of my mystical experiences in Jerusalem and its neighboring valleys – the Kidron and the Hinnom valleys. As they are unlike anything I have ever heard or read about, it is something I cannot explain. So it is for the reader to decide what meaning they have for her or him. However, I will give some background to my choosing to go there when I did.

In May 2001, our children sent us to Tuscany as a gift for our 50th Anniversary. One of them accompanied us with her husband. It was in Orvieto and then on the road to Sienna that I had what I consider a mystical moment. In each case, I experienced having words come to mind that I did not see as associations (I am a psychoanalyst), but rather as thoughts coming from outside myself. I certainly did not hear anything.

The Cathedral in Oriveto is famous, in part, for the elaborate design of its main doors. The one on the right as you face the building has figures of devils pushing people down into hell's fires using long handled pitchforks. As I stood looking at the scene, words came to me to the effect that they, the devils, were well known and had been so either forever or for a very long time. They are to be taken seriously.

On a drive to Sienna from the villa we were staying in just outside of Lucignano, the following words came to me. That my work on shame and rejection was worthwhile, and I should persist in studying them or words to that effect.

After our return from Italy, I gave some thought to what I have just described but not a great deal.

As the summer of 2001 began, I found a very somber mood developed in me. The mood was also one of anxiety as I began to think of something very bad happening in New York City where I was working. I lived on East 86th Street at Madison Avenue and had my office on the corner of East 86th Street and Park Avenue. When I thought about what might happen, I saw it as happening somewhere downtown. As the days went by, the mood changed to one of foreboding. In August, my wife and I went to the family cottage in Ontario, but this in no way provided any relief. In fact, we decided to renew our Canadian passports and to open a savings account in the small village nearby. All of this was done with an increasing sense of urgency.

On the morning of 9/11, I was eating breakfast in the New Amity Restaurant which is on Madison Avenue between East 84th and East 85th Streets when an announcement on the radio reported that a plane had crashed into one of the World Trade Towers. I did not think it was serious because I believed that once before a small plane had crashed into one, and previous to that a plane had crashed into the Empire State Building, I believe in the 1940's, so I finished eating and walked over to my office. I was not there long before I got a call from my daughter who lives in SoHo saying that the World Trade Centers had been completely destroyed. I was shocked, of course, but I was not surprised.

I believed there would be more attacks, and I became very anxious to the degree that I was really frightened. At that point the words 'Wales Forever' came strongly to mind. I believe that the words were not new to me, but the suddenness and force involved startled me. I decided then to go to a fancy grocery store at East 74th Street and Madison Avenue knowing that they sold Welsh Tynant spring water. After buying four bottles, I proceeded to walk south to SoHo to leave them at my daughter and son-in-law's place.

What I still remember clearly were the crowds of people walking north. It was a mild and sunny day. The sky was a deep blue without any clouds, and the air was very still. All public transportation had come to a halt and there were few cars to be seen. It was profoundly peaceful. I dropped the water off and continued to walk towards the site of the wreckage. A few blocks away, I was stopped by a police barrier, so I never got to see any of it that day. I did see a group of Salvation Army workers passing through the barrier as they hurried along in the direction of what was left of the buildings that had been destroyed.

I would never have guessed that the words 'Wales Forever' would have come to me so forcefully that morning. Some family history may be relevant.

My mother's great-grandfather and my father's great-grandfather were brothers. They were British army veterans of the Napoleonic wars and both moved to Lower Canada where they were given land grants in an area known as the Eastern Townships. My mother once told me that her grandmother, who had raised her as her mother had died, told her how she used to bathe her father's feet in olive oil when he came in from the fields at night. They had been frostbitten in Spain in the Peninsular War. The brothers were Welsh.

JERUSALEM

As the weeks went by following 9/11, I found myself thinking more and more about Jerusalem. If Tuscany was the mystical place I thought it was, then how much more so would Jerusalem be?

In February, 2002, I went there. The first time I went Swiss Air with a stopover in Zurich. Leaving the air terminal to begin the flight to Tel Aviv, a Swiss armored car, for security, went ahead of us out to where we took off. It was on the return flight that our flight path took us over Northern Quebec. I was in business class for the trip using miles I had saved. After that one trip, I always went economy. Also I began to use El Al as it flies direct from JFK to Tel Aviv which I find easier. I did go by Lufthansa two or three times and once on Turkish Air. The former goes by way of Frankfurt, and the latter goes by way of Istanbul.

On arriving in Ben Gurion airport that is just outside of Tel Aviv, I always took a van, called a cheroot, to Jerusalem. A van carries ten passengers and always takes a different route through the city as people are let off at their homes or at hotels. The result is that you enter the city by so many different ways that you get a good idea of just how large and modern it is.

On the first trip, I chose to stay at St. Andrew's Scots Memorial Church and Guest House. I read about it in a travel guide and knew it had an attractive garden, which it does.

I would guess that the guest house is about a mile from the Jaffa Gate which is probably the best known of all the gates of the Old City. The view from the parking area in front of the guest house is truly spectacular. In front and to the left is the head of the Hinnom Valley with the entire west wall of the Old City clearly visible beyond. To the right is Mount Zion with the Church of the Dormition. Further yet, one can sometimes see the Mountains of Moab which lie to the east of the Dead Sea. More often than not they are obscured by dust.

Returning from the direction of the Jaffa Gate towards the guest house, one easily identifies it from the flag of Scotland, showing the Cross of Saint Andrew, flying from the flagstaff atop the tower.

I have stayed at the guest house most trips. I did stay at St. George's Cathedral Guest House on three occasions. It is near to the Garden Tomb and the Damascus Gate which is in the north wall of the Old City. I settled on St. Andrew's because it is easier to get down into the Hinnom Valley by 4:00 a.m., which I try to do each day when I am in Jerusalem.

Early in my trips to Jerusalem, which I did every three months, I came to accept two facts that need to be attended to at this point. The first is that I believe a palm tree marks the site of His crucifixion. It is located down the road from the Jaffa Gate and is about twenty feet from a retaining wall next to the sidewalk. The road is the Hebron Road, but it is called the Jerusalem Brigade Road at that point. There is no other palm tree in sight. The reasons are many for seeing the palm tree as marking the site, but I will not go into them at this point. Its importance in this story will become apparent. The second fact is that the Garden Tomb, owned by a society in London, England, is in fact His tomb. In part I believe this because of a discussion I had with an American who had just been on a dig near the Garden Tomb. He said a tomb of a wealthy man was found nearby and is said to be that of Joseph of Arimathea.

So these two facts were my markers and have always remained so. I know that both are said to have taken place in the Church of the Holy Sepulchre. In this regard, I trust what I am saying will probably be ignored.

What is important is that an untold number of pilgrims have entered the Church of the Holy Sepulchre believing He died and was buried there. That is what makes it Holy.

Across the road from the palm tree is a small park, a grove of trees, and a deep bowl shaped area called the Sultan's Pool. The pool is often set up with hundreds of chairs to supply seating for various concerts, and it is probably the size of a football field. The park, the trees, and the Sultan's Pool together make up the head of the Hinnom Valley. It is a place of great significance in Judaism, as it is given as one of the gates of Hell in the Talmud. The other two gates consist of one in the depths of the oceans and the other in the Sinai where Korah and his followers were swallowed up in the earth for rebelling against Moses.

The site of the gate of hell in the Hinnom Valley has a long history. The Jebusites are said to have sacrificed children to Molloch there before the city was captured by the Hebrews. One recent tradition tells of young Orthodox students running past this place in fear as underground fires continued to smolder, and smoke was seen rising from cracks in the earth. It was once used as a dump and had fires burning in it.

It was probably in 2004 that my life in Jerusalem became a fixed pattern. I would get up at 2:45 a.m., leave the guest house at 3:45 a.m. and arrive across the road from the palm tree at 4:00 a.m. I would pick up any litter that I could fit into a plastic bag, there was usually one to be found, and throw away butts that were on the sidewalk, of which there were many, all in sight of the palm tree. This occupied me until 6:00 a.m. during which time I often sat on the wall bordering the sidewalk. Then from 6:00 a.m. to 7:00 a.m. I would sit or walk in the grove of trees and in the park until it was 7:00 a.m. when I walked back to the guest house for breakfast.

Much of the day I rested and read. I watched sports on Sky, so I began to get quite interested in soccer. Twice during my stay I would take a bouquet of white flowers to Mary's Tomb, which is near the head of the Kidron Valley. Once during my stay I would walk to Mea Sharim, an old Jewish quarter north and west of the Old City, where I would deliver a message. Finally, most days would find me in the German Colony, an area of shops and restaurants, about a half mile from the guest house and very European.

In 2005, I cannot be sure of the date, my life in Jerusalem changed in remarkable ways. One morning I was in the grove of trees about 7:00 a.m. when a man appeared walking up the path. He came up to me and said something to the effect of: "What is this about Jesus Christ?" There was no one else to be seen. I became very uncomfortable and not knowing what else to say, I chose to answer him by pointing out that He had been crucified where the palm tree stood. He responded to this by saying we should go over and examine the site. I said that I could not do that, while at the same time thinking there was no way I would do such a thing. He then suggested we sit down on a nearby bench and talk. Again I said I would not do that. I was feeling very intimidated, yet he had given me no reason to feel that way. Finally he asked me the direction to the path that leads up to Mount Zion. I showed it to him, and he left. He was very good looking, about five feet ten inches, black hair, cleanly shaven, and wore a clean black suit. It could have been similar to a military cadet's uniform as worn by Royal Military College cadets in Kingston, Ontario or, I presume, as worn at Sandhurst. However, he had no buttons or markings on his suit. His collar might have been loosened, but in every way he was immaculately dressed. A more pleasant person I have never met.

It was possibly the next day about the same time when another man appeared in the same place. He too wanted to talk. He was dusty, somewhat disheveled and asked if I could help him as he had no work. I suggested he might go over to the Damascus Gate to see if he could find work with a wholesaler. I then gave him ten shekels, but he showed no interest in leaving. Living in New York City at the time and encountering many homeless men left me feeling I had done what I could so why didn't he leave. I asked when someone had last given him ten shekels. He looked at me as if accepting my point and then left. He could not have been more pleasant, and yet, I was very intimidated by him, and I tried hard not to show it. I had the thought that everything I said or did was being evaluated and I must get things right. I felt the same way with the first man but even more so. In other words, get something right or do nothing and say nothing.

I cannot remember all of the events that occurred on my visits to Jerusalem.

However, I well recall that I took a break from visiting the city between February, 2006, and February, 2008. It was very good that I did so as I worked hard in New York, and I was able to pay off a good deal of debt in those two years. What follows took place in February, 2006, on my last visit before the break.

It was in the grove of trees, across the road from the palm tree, and between 7:00 a.m. and 8:00 a.m., when five huge black hounds came racing into the grove from the Sultan's Pool. Each was completely jet black, close to four feet tall and ran about close together in a wave-like motion. They ran about, one could say, in formation, leaping and bounding and, in short, having an absolute ball.

A woman came by walking her dog which was not on a leash. It was of medium size but nothing the size of the hounds. As soon as it saw them, it ran after them wanting to join in the fun. They ran off down the hill to the Pool area and were lost from view. I yelled at it to come back. Her dog came back, but I knew it was not because I had yelled at it. Rather I knew that they had run off leaving it behind because they had shown absolutely no interest in it when I had seen them together.

However, they were not gone for good, for at 5:00 a.m. the next day they showed up again. It was pitch dark, and no person or car was to be seen anywhere. I was on the sidewalk, across from the palm tree, when I first saw them. I chose to walk up to an archway over the sidewalk. It is part of an artists' colony building, and doing so gave me some feeling of being protected. I stood waiting. The dogs were similar to the ones I had seen the day before. They came down from Mount Zion and crossed the road to my side. This time they were walking, but the dogs were still close together. They barked, howled and snarled as they came up the sidewalk towards me. I became more and more anxious as they came nearer.

Fortunately, I had once been attacked by three small dogs while on vacation on Grand Bahama Island. I had learned from that experience that one will try to get behind you to bite you. This is what happened as one sidled up by the wall while the other four stopped about fifteen feet away. When it was about eight feet away, I drew myself up as much as I could in the archway, and in as a commanding a voice as I could muster, I said "Go away." He stared at me, and I stared back at him. It seemed like a long time, but I am sure it was just a few moments. Slowly he turned back and rejoined the others. They seemed to be circling around making a lot of noise, but then the dogs went off down the hill. For a time I thought of them as the hounds of hell but later that they were hounds of heaven.

Prior to that morning I had always felt safe in Jerusalem. Nothing had ever happened to leave me feeling anxious much less stressed out. But this experience left me feeling very anxious. Even during the Second Intifada, I had not felt this way.

This was not the end of the story as far as the hounds were concerned. Later that same day about 1:00 p.m., I was returning from Mary's Tomb by way of the road that follows the southeast corner of the Temple Mount. At one point the road is above a grove of olive trees, and the sidewalk has a wall and a railing on top. I leaned over the railing to look at the trees. About a hundred feet below me, I saw five black hounds similar to the ones I had seen that morning.

As soon as they spied me leaning over the railing, they set up the same loud barking and howling. Needless to say, I was very surprised, and I backed away from the railing. When I did so, the barking stopped, and I wondered what to do next. I was worried that they would come after me, but I never saw them again.

I continued on my way to the Dung Gate knowing there were usually police or soldiers or both there. Once inside the gate, I went up to the plaza in front of the Western Wall of the Temple Mount and stood there not knowing what to do. Then, as if I was suddenly connected to a party line, I experienced a man's voice. He was reminding someone that a person's health would need to be looked after during the two years he would be away. It was as if I was then disconnected as I heard nothing more. The line had gone dead.

I decided to leave Jerusalem for two years based on the man's conversation with another party. I left that day or the next as scheduled, so it was not until February, 2008 when I was back.

Since returning, I have followed the same routine as outlined previously. I now arrive Monday afternoon at the guest house and leave the following Monday evening. My 4:00 a.m. visits to the Hinnom Valley have continued unchanged.

My last trip was in May, 2010. I chose not to go in February, 2010 as we moved to Ithaca in January, and I needed to be home.

———

In Jerusalem over the last two years, I have met a number of men I think of as messengers. One may have been African, and the others were not. As I mentioned previously, I am immediately on the defensive when I meet them. All of them behaved as if they knew me or knew that I was the person they were looking for. One asked if I remembered him, and I said that I did. I always felt I was being tested in some way or other.

I believe it was in 2008 when I saw the first man I had met two years before in the grove of trees. He was standing at the corner where the gate to St. Andrew's is located. I knew he saw me coming up the hill towards him, but he continued to ask for money from people passing by. I heard him say he had no living wife and four or five children to care for. Only one man in a group of five or six men gave him some money.

When I got to where he was, I said I had no change, but I was going over to the German Colony, and I would give him some when I came back. I went there and had something to eat. When I got back to the corner, he was gone. I have to admit I was somewhat relieved not to find him. When I think of him now, it is hard to believe I did not give him a bank note, but I did not. Was I simply being cheap, or am I that defensive when in the company of one of these men? I guess it's both as well as my living in New York.

The second man I had met within the grove of trees two years before I met at least one more time. About midday near the palm tree, and possibly on my way to the Jaffa Gate, I was sitting on a low wall when he came up to me. He was the one who asked if I remembered him. At first, for a brief moment, I did not, but then I did. For some reason a thought flashed through my mind that he had changed in appearance to someone I remembered. I may have given him ten shekels as I had done before, but I do not remember it if I did or not. Again, he could not have been nicer.

The gate of St. Andrews is at the top of a hill that leads down to the Cinématèque. In August 2009, I walked down to have supper there. It was about 5:30 p.m. and the street was empty. Suddenly a slightly built man about five feet six inches tall ran down a flight of stairs from the park above. I knew he had been waiting for me as he came straight over to me and asked me to buy some chewing gum. He showed me a box of it in a leather satchel he had slung over his shoulder. He was demanding, and I said I didn't want any, feeling put upon. As he kept insisting, I began to think of the man who I said I would give change to when I came back from the German Colony, and he had left before I returned. So I told this man I would get a box, but I had to eat first. I told him I would be back by 6:30 p.m. This seemed to satisfy him, and I went down to supper. Once in the restaurant, I ordered and then soon realized I might miss this man too. Certainly I could not eat a main course and get back to where he was by 6:30 p.m.

I ate some soup but came close to having a panic attack at the thought of missing him. I paid the bill and I said I would be back to finish my meal. I went up to meet him, and when I saw him, I was much relieved. He was crouched down examining a small bush with tiny white blossoms. He seemed to be totally engrossed in what he was doing. This seemed strange, and it must also have been to a cyclist who had stopped to talk with him but left before I got there.

I handed him a fifty shekel note and took the box of gum. He then offered me other things indicating his satchel, but it appeared to be empty when he then half opened it. I said that I did not want anything else.

I asked him where he was from, and he

pointed to an address in Saudi Arabia that was printed on the back of the box of gum. Finally I asked him if he was a Jew, a Muslim, or a Christian. He answered: "I have no religion." As I walked away I thought: "Well, you've got that right. Messengers would have no earthly religion."

The last man that I encountered who I believed was a messenger was in November of 2009. One morning, a Tuesday, I went out the front door of the guest house after finishing breakfast. The area for cars is in front of the door, and it was pretty well clear of cars at that moment. At once, I noticed a tall, erect, dark-skinned man standing at the edge of the area directly in front of the door. He was wearing a trench coat and a fedora, and he was facing the Old City. He was singing. I stopped to watch him as he began to talk to some women who had come for a meeting in the guest house. I became concerned for them as they seemed uncomfortable talking to him. I went over to him and asked if he would like some water. When I did so, the women promptly left. However, he said he would like some, and I got a cup of water from the office. When I handed it to him, he told me to put it on the curb in a way that irritated me, so I told him to do it himself.

At this point I went over to where there was a wicker chair and sat in it to read my Bible. He stopped singing and came over to where I was and said he needed to speak to me. I asked him how long it would take, and he said not long. He was very nice about it.

He produced a book from somewhere on his person. He then produced a cane and put the book on it. Both the book and the cane were not to be seen on him before this. The book did not seem like a book but more like an appearance of one. On the cover were the words "The Temple" and just below the words "The Messiah." He asked me who was the Messiah, and I said Jesus Christ. This seemed to satisfy him, and I went back to my reading. That was the only time I was ever in the parking area with my Bible.

The next day I saw him again. He was standing in the same spot as the day before, and again he was singing. I really yelled a "Good morning" to him, and he gave no sign of recognition. I was still angry at him. However, I think he got back at me a few minutes later when a bird targeted my shoulder. That had never happened before.

The most remarkable thing about him was that his upper teeth protruded at right angles to his upper gums. They were absolutely parallel to the ground he was standing on. I could see why the women he talked with had been so uncomfortable. He clearly had reason to be irritable, and I had no reason to be so quick to take offense.

It was on that same trip that, standing next to the Kotel, the Western Wall, I had the words: "Have faith in the good" come to me. They are words that I treasure.

I may have met messengers in New York

City since working there. When I met these men, and they were all men, their clothes seemed unremarkable, and I usually had no discomfort when talking with them. One stopped me for directions to a jewelry store on Madison Avenue at a point where I myself needed to go there. However, one man was unique.

Tom stood for many years under a theatre canopy between Lexington Avenue and Park Avenue on the north side of 86th Street. He was always singing unless someone, usually a woman, had stopped to talk with him. He called me Tom without ever asking my name. I had met him a year or two before 9/11. When I saw him, I always said "Hello" and gave him a dollar.

Tom's skin was very brown, and for a long time I thought he was an African, but I cannot tell. He had aquiline features and bore himself with dignity, but in overall behavior he was like no one I had ever seen before. He was always singing, and a person I knew said he had a good tenor voice. He was six feet tall or more and always wore a fedora. In cold weather he wore a trench coat and leather gloves which clearly was not enough as he often looked to be very cold. He was usually absent in January and February.

Always friendly, we usually just chatted about the weather. I believe I told him when I went to Jerusalem or had been there. Only once did I see him off his station. He was walking down Lexington Avenue with a box of what appeared to be Godiva chocolates. Another time, it was closer to 11:00 p.m., I heard him singing on East 86th Street but going in that direction he was nowhere to be seen.

I said he was always very erect, but in the last several years, he has become very stooped and leans on a cane, which he always carries with him.

It always seemed that Tom's presence a few doors from my office had something to do with me, and I wondered if he was monitoring me in some way or other.[1] I know when I first saw him twelve years ago, I was across East 86th Street from where I could see him standing, and I did not want to meet him. I did avoid him for a few weeks until we met and probably shook hands. I felt with him the same way I have felt with the messengers, very awkward and very determined to be careful about what I said or did. I have wondered if he was the same man as the one who asked me who the Messiah was.

---

[1] I recently found a diary entry for February 3, 2001, that might explain this.
"On December 12, 2000, at 5:45 p.m., I met Tom under the theatre marquee on 86th Street at Lexington Avenue. He looked the same as ever. However, while looking at him face-to-face, a pitch black oval with two white orbs replaced his face. I said 'I think you are in league with the devil.' To which he replied, 'Is that what you think?'"

THE KOTEL IN JERUSALEM

The Western Wall of the Temple Mount, sometimes spoken of as the Wailing Wall, is called the Kotel by the Jews. They believe that the Divine Presence, The Shekinah, rests on top of it. Christians speak of the Divine Presence as the Holy Spirit but see it as part of the Holy Trinity hence present throughout the world, and not particularly related to the Temple Mount. Jesus laid great emphasis on the Divine Presence, the Holy Spirit. He made the point that if one blasphemed it, then there would be bad if not terrible consequences. I believe He would have thought of it as resting on top of the Temple Mount.

I have gone to the Kotel many times, usually following my visits to Mary's Tomb in the upper end of the Kidron Valley. The time I experienced a conversation, at least one side of it, I did not feel singled out. But on two different occasions I did feel that I had been. The first, possibly in 2003 or 2004, was when I received a Bronx cheer as I entered the plaza area. I did not actually hear it, but it came to me in my thoughts and was not an association! I find it amazing, but I can smile about it. I do not know why I was given one, but I have no trouble figuring out why I deserved one. The second was when the words "Have faith in the good" came to me.

———

Each time I have visited Jerusalem I have taken a bouquet of flowers down to Mary's Tomb in the Kidron Valley. From the guest house I go down into the Hinnom Valley and then up to the Jaffa Gate to a flower shop behind a hotel. The lady gives me a large bouquet of white flowers. She then asks, "To Mary's Tomb?" to which I answer, "Yes." I then walk up the road past Saint James Armenian Church and continue along inside the wall until I reach the Dung Gate. Then I go down a long walk with many steps to the floor of the Kidron Valley where I walk past James's Tomb and Absalom's Pillar. My path then takes me up to the road that fronts Mary's Tomb.

I deliver the flowers to one of the monks who sees that they are put in a water-filled vase and placed on an altar next to the tomb itself. I have tried to do this twice each visit as a tribute to my mother, my wife, and all mothers. Needless to say, it is a tribute to Mary.

Before I recount what happened one day, I need to go back to the day before. I had walked to Mea Sharim and decided to walk back the way I had come. Entering the southern part of King George Street, I found the sidewalk filled with people walking in both directions. Looking up, I saw a person about fifteen feet in front of me. The person had the most beautiful face I have ever seen. It seemed to be twice the size of any face I have a memory of, but it may in part have been the radiance of her smile. I smiled back and then looked down. A moment later I looked up, and she was perhaps eight feet away and still smiling in the same way. Again I looked down, and the next time I looked I saw a woman facing the same direction as I was walking. Turning my head to the right as I walked past, I could only see the left side of her face. It was of normal size, and she was no longer smiling. The face could have been that of my oldest sister when she was sixty years old or thereabouts. Needless to say, I blamed myself for the fact she was no longer smiling.

Her head and part of her upper neck did not seem unusual but below that a black cloth fell straight down, which would have seemed so. But with so many people around us and people walking so fast, no one seemed to even notice her. I said nothing to her. Although I keep saying "her," I believe it was an angel and thus giving it a gender would be inappropriate.

Most important, I saw this encounter as a "heads up" for what was to come the next day.

Mary's Tomb is fifty feet or more below the level of a small plaza outside the doors of the building that houses the tomb. The plaza is often filled with tourist groups led by tour guides. I have never seen a monk or a nun in the plaza in all of the times I have walked across it. Sometimes it is empty, but in recent years it is usually a busy place with tour groups and the ever present men selling religious souvenirs.

On this visit, with a bouquet of lilies and white flowers,[2] I went down the steps from the road into the plaza to find it deserted.

As I approached the doors, I found two women sitting side by side at my left. Both wore long robes of brown and black with hoods and were sitting erect. I took a fraction of a second to look at their faces and then looked away. They looked pleasant enough, but I could not describe either one. I instantly felt that the older woman was the one I should give the flowers to and not enter the building with them. I crossed myself and put the flowers in her outstretched arms. I turned and walked down, perhaps fifty steps, to the tomb. When I came back up a few minutes later, the two women were still there. This time the younger woman was leaning against the older one. There was radiant love surrounding them. I gave a little wave as I walked past.

The next time I went to the tomb the plaza was once again empty. I took the bouquet

---

[2] The shopkeeper had added lilies without my asking. That had never happened before.

down to the monk and then came back up. In front of me was an African woman, very black, in robes of white, emerald green, and black. She was sitting next to the stairs at the end of the plaza which lead up to the right and the road. I felt totally at ease with her, and I put twenty-six shekels into her cupped hands. I touched her arm as I left her to walk up the stairs.

All three women were seated in the most relaxed position they could have wished. The fact is that there was nothing to sit on where I encountered them.

PRAY FOR THE PEACE OF JERUSALEM

On my very first visit to Jerusalem, I took a taxi from Mary's Tomb to the German Colony. The driver told me, when asked, that he was a Muslim. So I asked him why he had not moved to the U.S. or to Chile. He had told me he was married and had two or three children. His answer, taken at face value, mirrors my own deepest sense of what Jerusalem means to me. He said: "I believe that when there is peace in Jerusalem there will be peace in the world."

My last trip to Jerusalem was in May of 2010. I followed the same routines of previous trips. Nothing unusual happened until I arrived at 4:00 a.m. Saturday morning at the palm tree. It was Shabbat, and I had resolved not to pick up any litter. However, I saw three large pieces of trash directly across from the palm tree. My first thought was not to pick them up as I had promised myself I would not. But because they were where they were, I did so anyway. Immediately a crow or a rook near the base of the palm tree set up a dreadful din. I became very anxious as I knew at once it did so because I had broken my promise.

I then remembered what Simon Peter had said when Ananias and his wife lied about the amount of money they had received from the sale of their property. No one had told them to sell their property much less donate all the proceeds to the community. Likewise no one had asked me to keep Shabbat as the seventh day. It had been entirely my idea.

In the case of Ananias and his wife, both had dropped dead when confronted with their lies. Both had experienced a profound rejection. In each, one sees such a toxic degree of physical pain that the ventricle of the heart must have expanded to such a degree as to cause instant death.

This rejection of Ananias and his wife in the Book of Acts is an excellent example of what can happen when someone is suddenly rejected. In the Talmud the story of Bar Kamsa is also one of sudden rejection and is well known to every Yeshiva student.

On this trip I realized finally that I must be far more focused on doing what I say I am going to do.

———————

In every situation where I have experienced rejection it has been for my own good. An example is the two year hiatus in taking trips to Jerusalem. Those years with no travel expenses allowed me to pay off all my unsecured debt. This was accomplished just prior to the subprime mortgage debacle.

The critical encounter was with the man who showed me the book on the front of which were the words: "The Temple" and "The Messiah." I needed to say simply that Jesus Christ is the Messiah.

EPILOGUE

I n Leonard Susskind's book, *The Black Hole War,*[3] he discusses the Holographic Principle. It is well worth reading in its entirety. Simply stated, it says that what we experience as concrete reality may well be a hologram, and the holograph is stored on strings possibly at the edge of the universe. He suggests that what is stored on the strings could be drawn into the hologram by a secret code.

In the light of what has been told about Jerusalem, is the secret code reciprocity of love and wisdom from heaven and faith and service from this world? I believe there is a monitoring of faith and service. Is the monitoring sometimes benign and sometimes more strident?

———————

"Ask and it shall be given you; seek and ye shall find; knock, and it shall be open unto you.

---

[3] Susskind Leonard: *The Black Hole War,* Back Bay Books (2009)

For every one that asketh receiveth; and he that seeketh findeth; and to him that knocketh it shall be opened."

Matthew 7: 7, 8

AFTERWORD

I s there a fifth dimension where time as we
understand it does not exist? I believe so.